SOLVING AMERICA'S DEBT AND DEFICIT

ROGER H. EWING

SOLVING AMERICA'S DEBT AND DEFICIT

ISBN-13: 978-1461139119
ISBN-10: 1461139112

Library of Congress #: 2011906998

Printed by: CreateSpace

Printed in the United States of America

Dedicated to the American People

This book is an attempt to help solve America's Debt and Deficit. The author, Roger Ewing, has many years experience in solving problems as he served as a Management Consultant to over 300 companies.

OTHER PUBLISHED BOOKS

"It is Written the Shocking Downfall of the USA"
— 2009

This book is a wakeup call to alert Americans that if the United States Congress does not begin to face reality the events of this book may come to pass. The book predicts that the year 2011 is a critical year for the Middle East. It seems the prediction has come true.

"Powerful Guide to Living the Good Life" — 1998

Subject of Masters Degree Thesis was "How to Solve a Problem"
Received an A+ from the University of Southern California. —1970

Table of Contents

INTRODUCTION

$14,000,000,000,000 IS $14 TRILLION
DOLLARS no matter how you write it! And
it is growing every day! Responsible people
would never have put our country in peril.
Spending continues at a record pace. Soon
we could be at $15 TRILLION DOLLARS.

The percentage of the national debt to the
Gross Domestic Product, (GDP), on an
annualized basis is growing at a record level
not seen since World War II. During World
War II the national debt ratio to the GDP
was 120%. Only through a Republican party
controlled Congress in 1947 which
implemented severe spending cuts the USA
was able to get out of a severe financial
situation.

One fact that stands out about 1946 was that
47% of American workers were employed
by government. In 1947 government
employment was drastically reduced by
10%.

In 2010 government employment exceeded 50%. Government employment has been steadily increasing as private employment has steadily decreased.

How do we reduce our national debt? It will require a combination of intelligent and patriotic decisions. We will need to increase our private employment. We will need to decrease our federal spending. This will have immediate short term benefits as well as long term benefits. This will set our country on a course of prosperity that we have not experienced in decades.

We reduced our national debt under former President Bill Clinton ONLY because he had a Republican congress that would not spend foolishly and because he saved billions by reducing our active duty military by 25%. President Clinton was out to make a name for himself and leave a positive legacy after his Monica scandal which almost got him impeached. His lack of concern for our national defense during his eight years in office saw several hundred Americans attacked and killed. This led to our enemies correctly perceiving a weakened America resulting and climaxing with the 9/11 attacks. For a detailed analysis of our weakened military and national defense I urge you to read my last book, "It is Written the Shocking Downfall of the USA".

This time we can reduce our debt and we can do it right and not at the mercy of weakening our military and national defense. This time we can reduce our debt and strengthen our military and national defense.

Our national debt is based on the spending by our Congress in relation to our economic production. Simply, if the Congress spends more than our government takes in that creates a debt. It is like a family that spends more than they earn which in time may result in bankruptcy as a family cannot print any money.

Senator Kent Conrad stated in the Senate

Budget Committee hearing on March 8, 2011, "USA's federal spending is the highest in the last 60 years and USA's revenue is the lowest in the last 60 years". Yet Senator Conrad voted against reducing the deficit by 1.6% on March 9, 2011.

Senator Jeff Sessions said, "debt in the USA will be 100% of GDP by the end of FY 2011".

Senator Tom Coburn stated on March 9, 2011, "$4.5 Billion Dollars is added to the USA deficit every day".

America borrows 40 cents of every dollar that is spent.

Erskine Bowles and Allan Simpson who headed up President Obama's Federal Deficit Commission suggested $4 Trillion Dollars in reductions over 10 years. So far President Obama has ignored their recommendations. He offered one trillion dollars over ten years but even that according to economists has some "voodoo" math.

President Obama increased discretionary spending by 24% in his first two years.

Republicans offered to cut the deficit by $61Billion Dollars on March 9, 2011 which is 1.6 % of the deficit. The Democrats voted against doing that.

The average age of a republic is 207 years. Every republic in history failed over fiscal issues – not because they were attacked from an outside enemy. America is on the brink of failure. Yet on March 9, 2011 Democratic members offered to cut only $4.7 Billion Dollars out of $3.73 Trillion Dollars which is one-half of one percent of the federal budget for FY 2011.

These are troubling times for the United States of America. It's a quagmire. Are we at the abysmal end of the greatest idea of government the world has ever witnessed? The idea of a truly democratic government is where the people have individual rights. Those individual rights are spelled out in a constitution that is transparent to any and all to see and read. Those individual rights fueled the independence of the individual spirit to create, develop and implement the largest and most effective economy of success in the world. That success became so powerful that it has dominated the world politic since the end of World War II.

The majority of the American people have not paid attention to the many elected politicians who want to completely transform our great country to a second or third rate power. This movement called the Progressive movement has finally reached its pinnacle as President, Barack Obama, has appointed his Progressive friends to top levels of running the government. President Obama has appointed thirty czars to help him transform America. A number of these czars have a history of hostility toward America.

This movement in part is based on the redistribution of wealth. The goal of this redistribution of wealth is to take from the rich and give to the poor. This dangerous philosophy is not only to enact this principle to our country but throughout the whole world.

Is this the beginning of the end of America? Does anyone know if this is our time to fall from within as many of the other great dynasties? The character, Sydney Carton, in "A Tale of Two Cities" said, "This is the best of times this is the worst of times if we only knew what to do?" Friends, our best of times has eroded and we may not get them back. Knowledgeable preachers are saying these are the last days. The Bible says the last days are chaotic. These days are definitely chaotic.

The Durants, Will and Ariel, may have said it best in their volumes of civilizations, many scholars have called their work the "Great Books". In short their important message was HISTORY REPEATS ITSELF. The author will offer his suggestions on lowering and eliminating the federal debt and federal deficit. We need to understand that our national debt, national deficit, jobs, and the economy are interrelated. A change in one area may create a change in the other areas. Any realistic and responsible lowering of our federal deficit will involve our federal employees who are for the most part represented by unions. These federal government employees, along with their counterparts in state, county, and city governments, comprise more than 50% of the American workforce. They on the average earn more than their counterparts in the private sector. Their benefits are two or three times more especially the pensions and the private sector pays the bill. With the federal deficits growing every day this has become a huge problem. And the states have the same problem, 45 out of 50 states are in the red. The union leadership does not want to lose any of their union employees because they want those union dues which finance among other things the liberal political campaigns which in turn are a vicious cycle of feeding each other's agendas.

We will tackle the battle between the unions and their representatives, the Democratic Party, versus the taxpayers which could become AMERICA'S SECOND CIVIL WAR.

Before we go there we will discuss some financial issues.

BEN BERNANKE VERSUS NEW VARIABLES

Chairman of the Federal Reserve, Ben Bernanke, is very intelligent and knowledgeable about most matters financial. The author has listened to him many times thanks to C-SPAN broadcasting the many congressional committee hearings.

Dr. Bernanke testified on March 2, 2011 that reducing the federal budget by $60 Billion Dollars for the FY 2011 was satisfactory with him. He commented that the sooner we get started on federal budget cuts the better we can begin on a long term solution to our deficit. It was mentioned that the U. S. Congress does not do long term budgets or budget planning. It would be easy for the Congress to do a long term budget estimate but in reality most of the Congress may not be around long enough to implement those budgets and it would be therefore just a way of "kicking the can down the road" on any

meaningful cuts. In other words why should
the present Congress deal with cuts now when
future Congresses can do it later which has
been what has been happening. Ben Bernanke
is correct as long term planning is the ideal but
the ideal is rarely accomplished.

Bernanke is an expert authority on the Great
Depression. His efforts have focused on trying
to get our economy growing at a rate that
increases our economy and private sector
employment. One of his main concerns is to
keep inflation under 2%. If inflation were to
rise above 2%, rising interest rates may create
a slow down in the economy plus a sharp
increase in the loan payments we make to
China and our other lenders of our debt.

It is important to note that there are a number
of different variables in play this time
compared to the Great Depression. During the
Great Depression we did not have a federal
deficit of over $14 Trillion Dollars. Second, we
did not have a global economy an economy
which is highly dependent on countries
exports and imports. Third, back in the 1930s
we did not have two rapidly growing

economies with such large populations, China and India competing against us. Their labor forces are happy to have jobs even if their pay scales are much lower than U. S. standards.

Fourth, the Great Depression ended in the USA with the robust manufacturing for the war goods for World War II but in today's deep recession we have already been in two wars for at least eight years without an increase in manufacturing but rather a drain on our budgets. Fifth, in the 1930s we did not have constant terrorist threats in the USA. Sixth, no country in the 1930s had a nuclear weapon, either strategic or tactical. Seventh, when we were attacked in 1941 we had time to recoup but today if we would be attacked by a considerable enemy the odds are we would not have time to recoup. Everything today is so much faster. We need to be right 100% of the time and our enemy may need to be right just once.

Eighth, we did not have a housing crisis. According to First American Core Logic, Inc. approximately 11 million or 23% of all residential properties with mortgages were in negative equity in the third quarter of 2010. According to the Mortgage Bankers Association National Delinquency Survey one out of seven borrowers was delinquent or in foreclosure during the 4th quarter of 2010. The total outstanding U. S. residential mortgage debt was estimated at $11.5 Trillion Dollars as of September 30, 2010.

Most economists believe the main obstacles to the housing recovery are a weak labor market, weak demand for homes, elevated vacancy and foreclosure rates and the strengthened lending standards.

Therefore Dr. Bernanke, there is a lot more at stake today with many more variables than what we faced during the Great Depression. Dr. Bernanke, the author hopes that every-thing you are doing to fix our economy and our financial well being works and the sooner the better. In the author's opinion, we need to get America strong again before we solve all of the world's problems.

Some of the suggestions in this book may have a negative impact on some other countries for the short term especially in our trade, imports and exports. Also, the author believes in fixing our economy more rapidly that what he perceives were your comments to do it over 10 to 20 years as we may not have that long before something drastic may happen.

TWO MEASUREMENTS

The UNEMPLOYMENT RATE is a controversial number. It appears that all it does is measure the number of people laid off during a particular week and the number of new hires. It does NOT measure the number of people that are unemployed.

When the unemployment rate was 9.5% many economists said that the economy had to add 300,000 people a week to keep the rate at the present level. Anything over that number the rate would come down, but as the weeks went by and the economy did not come close to adding that amount the unemployment rate mysteriously came down. There surely must be a better way.

The Bureau of Labor Statistics with all of their resources should be able to come up with a weekly number of people who are working full time. They could calculate how many people who are not working from the ages 18 to 65. Obviously they could deduct college students from their total based on a report from the colleges/universities.

The term UNDEREMPLOYED is a nebulous term and could represent anyone who thinks they are not satisfied with their employment status. The underemployed rate has been around 16% or higher this past year. Determining how many people are working part-time may be more difficult.

According to the Bureau of Labor Statistics, the most comprehensive measuring of the unemployment rate, which includes those working part-time who would rather work full time and those not looking for work but who want to work and are available for work (discouraged workers) was 16.7% in December 2010. This is close to the record high of 17.4% in October 2009.

The Consumer Price Index, CPI, can be misleading. It's a weighted index of seven categories. The housing category of the CPI is 42% of the index. According to the Consumer Expenditure Survey, housing is approximately 33% of actual consumer spending. Because the value of housing and the sales of houses has dropped sharply it dwarfs the real numbers of the CPI when all seven categories are combined. In 2011 food and gasoline prices are soaring. February 2011 food prices went up 3.9% and gasoline prices went up 4%. Vegetable prices have gone up 100% at the grocery stores. Gasoline prices have gone up over 50% in the last year. Commodity prices have soared with some commodities having risen 90%. Chairman Ben Bernanke in a recent congressional testimony stated that the inflation rate was only 1.2%.

The problem is if inflation rises then the federal government becomes obligated to raise social security payments as well as our debt payments to our lenders like China, Japan, Great Britain and others. This would devastate our deficit even further as this would increase our monthly payments dramatically. This Mr. Bernanke and the rest of us do not want.

Is it time that our United States Congress enter the 21st Century Information Age? For example, the Congressional Budget Office, (CBO), is considered to be non-partisan. They are given information, a bill, to provide an estimate on that information. If the information given to them is incomplete or false then their estimate is not complete and should be considered unreliable. The CBO was given information on Obamacare and they came up with an estimate. The CBO in reality are "robots" and not allowed to have the authority to use other information that they know would have greatly altered their estimate. The CBO was not allowed to incorporate the $300 Billion Dollars given to doctors which was an integral part which would have changed their estimate from a positive outcome to a negative one. Also, Secretary of Health and Human Services Kathleen Sebelius acknowledged on March 7, 2011 that the $500 Billion Dollars that was taken from Medicare and applied toward Obamacare was double counting. The $500

Billion Dollars was the important number which President Obama claimed reduced the health care costs. Change the authority of the CBO that "garbage in and garbage out" can be a thing of the past.

REVISITING GOLDMAN SACHS AND TARP

This author in revisiting the Troubled Asset Relief Program (TARP) bailout of September/October 2008 is having a hard time processing what really happened.

Henry Paulson prior to becoming Secretary of the Treasury was the CEO of Goldman Sachs. Paulson and Ben Bernanke, the Federal Reserve Chairman, went to President George W. Bush in September 2008 and said the sky is falling. They said without a bailout of our financial system the whole system will collapse now.

Not tomorrow but today. Therefore, any President receiving this information from these office holders had to believe they knew what they were talking about. President Bush got the support of Congress and approved $700 Billion Dollars which became called TARP.

Here is what the problem is. For the year 2006 Goldman Sachs claimed a profit of $9.34 Billion Dollars. As early as March 18, 2008 the Federal Reserve "loaned" actually through buying preferred stock, billions of dollars to Goldman Sachs. From March 18, 2008 to April 22, 2009 the Federal Reserve bought/loaned Goldman Sachs $589 Billion Dollars.

That's $589 Billion Dollars! How does anyone loan a corporation $589 Billion Dollars when the corporation has a profit of only $9 Billion Dollars? Or buy $589 Billion Dollars of preferred stock of a corporation that may file bankruptcy or be in deep financial trouble? They "must" have asked for the money meaning they were in need. But who couldn't use an extra $589 Billion Dollars?

The total amount of money Goldman Sachs "borrowed" through selling preferred stock was $782 Billion Dollars. They also sold their preferred stocks to others than the Federal Reserve.

Goldman Sachs made $2.3 Billion Dollars profit for the year 2008 and paid $10.9 Billion Dollars in employee pay and bonuses.

Goldman Sachs paid approximately 1% tax on their earnings.

Representative Lloyd Doggett (D-TX) said, "with the right hand begging for bailout money, the left is hiding it offshore".

Goldman Sachs has been involved in several controversies. The author lists two which may be of interest to the readers. On May 10, 2009 the Goldman Sachs Group agreed to pay $60 Million Dollars to end an investigation by the Massachusetts attorney general's office into whether the firm helped promote unfair home loans in the state. On July 15, 2010, Goldman Sachs agreed to pay $550 Million Dollars.

- $300 Million Dollars to the U.S. government
- $250 Million Dollars to investors – in a settlement with the SEC Security Exchange Commission in a civil fraud lawsuit.

The Bell System, American Bell Telephone Company was declared to have a monopoly. In 1984 a federal mandate broke up the company into separate companies.

The question is should Goldman Sachs be broken up and divided into separate companies? A lot of people panicked and declared Goldman Sachs too big to fail and had to be rescued.

FANNIE MAE AND FREDDIE MAC

The areas of the country which have been identified as having a higher percentage of residential mortgages under water or having a higher rate of foreclosures should have a moratorium on building permits. Builders of new homes are mobile and can build new homes in areas of the country that are not diluted. We don't need competition of building new homes in areas where the markets are flooded with too many resale or foreclosed homes.

The federal government provides the money for the most part to back residential mortgages. The U. S. Congress formed Fannie Mae and Freddie Mac as quasi-government entities to "manage" the monies which are taxpayer based and are funded mostly through the Federal Reserve. It has become apparent that Fannie Mae and Freddie Mac have not been able to adequately manage their mandate. There are various reasons for their failures including the U. S. Congress mandate starting in 1997 to provide financing money to banks and mortgage brokers to loosen the requirements for an individual to qualify for a loan. The enormous monies provided to Fannie Mae and Freddie Mac has created some problems including the excessive salaries and bonuses to their executives of millions of dollars. It's time to fully investigate both organizations.

It is suggested that the U. S. Congress create a new federal program controlled 100% by appointed expert people to "manage" the monies and funding of the housing market. This new program will phase out Fannie Mae and Freddie Mac's involvement in receiving federal money. Fannie and Freddie will dispense from funding any more residential loans based on a time table that will be established by the U. S. Congress. The new housing program will have new and effective guidelines to operate. The initial funding will be capped at $500 Billion Dollars.

The author was going to suggest that the Securities Exchange Commission, SEC, lawyers would monitor the transition period of phasing out Fannie Mae and Freddie Mac but after reconsideration the SEC needs to have someone monitor them after a number of their lawyers seem to monitor porn sites for extended periods of time. If these lawyers don't have enough work they should be let go. We will therefore need to find lawyers or other professionals who have integrity to do the monitoring of the phase down.

The millions of the foreclosed homes are a major problem. In theory the mortgage broker of a mortgage could renegotiate the loan with a borrower. But in reality once a mortgage broker approves a loan that loan may be sold to another broker who may resell it or co-mingle it with other loans for sale. Do we need to go back to basics and keep things simple? The originator of a loan should keep that loan. This may restore some responsibility in making and approving a loan if they have to keep it instead of selling it.

AMERICA'S SECOND CIVIL WAR?

AMERICA'S SECOND CIVIL WAR was and is caused by greed and thirst for power. It has been the greed of the spoiled public sector employees who now comprise over 50% of the work force that now has created a financial crisis. And it has been the power grab of the union leadership and their Democratic Party sponsors to implement their social agendas, the Progressive Movement.

This book makes an attempt to solve the financial problems, debt and deficit.

Have the union leaders and the union members gotten the message that they need to compromise in order to save their jobs? It doesn't appear that they have. For example, in 2010, in the aircraft industry, the union voted against ratifying a labor contract. The company clearly informed the union that their business was down and they had only a few new orders. The union members didn't care that their employer was struggling. The result was predictable. The company had no choice. They had to lay off 1000 union employees. The company in order to survive contacted the state and city for financial assistance. The debate centered on if the company could not obtain some financial assistance they would have to close their operations, lay off the existing employees, send some jobs overseas, and move to a better business environment. The city agreed to some tax incentives for the company and that kept the company from laying off their employees and from moving.

A company's first instinct is to survive. All companies need to make a profit to survive. When a company loses money and many have lost millions of dollars then all the employees need to face reality and work together.

Many Wall Street companies helped cause the financial crisis; the government bailed them out with taxpayers money. These Wall Street companies helped create the financial crisis and they were deemed too big to fail. General Motors and Chrysler also received a bailout. They also were deemed too big to fail. The General Motors bailout was very controversial. The bond holders normally are the first ones to receive some of the "pie" but in this case the federal government dismissed their first position in favor of the unions receiving approximately 60% of the stock. Shockingly within less than two years after receiving their federal bailouts some of the Wall Street companies and General Motors started handing out large bonuses to many of their employees. The money of those federal bailouts belonged to the American people, the taxpayers. These bailed out companies should not be allowed to pay out any bonuses until they have paid back ALL of the bailout money plus interest.

The great internal debate in the USA will be the labor unions and their Progressive supporters versus the American conservatives. The American conservatives want to save our country from financial ruin. The unions and the Progressives want to maintain their present wages and pensions. These union pensions in the public sector are for the most part unfunded and may destroy the financial security and the economy of our country. Selfish politicians gave public sector employees these huge pensions in hopes of being elected and reelected over and over again. There should be some way to hold these irresponsible politicians accountable. Should there be "fiduciary responsibility" in the public sector?

One of the untold stories of our time is the number of politicians who "bought" their elections by passing legislation that favored specific groups and then received large contributions from those advantaged by the legislation. There should be campaign laws against this.

These irresponsible politicians should be blamed for any coming riots and violence as the unions and their supporters take to the streets to threaten and antagonize anyone in the way from taking any part of their wages and lucrative pensions. It is theirs and they will defend what they were given with violence if need be. The names and photos of these irresponsible politicians should be sprawled over television sets. It is easy to look at the public records to determine who authorized giving away the public dough without the proper funding in place. Kicking the can down the road is no excuse. Most of these irresponsible politicians have already left their elected offices but the public, their friends and family can see their "mugs" on television if violence erupts.

Maybe, just maybe, there will be some SHAME. But don't count on it as SHAME doesn't seem to be an American trait anymore like it is in the Japanese culture. Rioting groups take a life of their own once they get started. It is almost inevitable that there will be burning of buildings and looting. Peaceful demonstrations can easily turn violent. All it takes are a few hotheads shooting either several police officers or innocent bystanders. There would more than likely be quick retaliation. Don't you think? How do you control a rioting mob?

President Obama made comments against Egypt's use of the police and army about using some force against the rioters there. This was after the rioters there had burned some buildings, and destroyed and stole some priceless artifacts from the museums, and injured several police. So was it okay for the rioters to do what they did and how do you stop that from continuing? President Obama also advised the Egyptian leaders to give in to the demands of the Egyptian protestors. And yet President Obama would not give into the demands of approximately 70% of the American people for nearly a year as he pushed his Obamacare through the Democratic Party controlled congress. Is President Obama a fine example of "do as I say but not as I do?" So the question becomes will President Obama call out the police or National Guard or army to quell any burning of property, looting or violence caused by union members? There will be a good chance these rioters will be armed with guns and rifles and there may be shootings. This may become AMERICA'S SECOND CIVIL WAR. Remember over 50% of workers in our country are public sector employees and for the most part their salaries and pensions are much higher than their private sector counterparts.

More than likely these government employees will fight to keep their "entitlements".

There are millions of Americans who have been out of work for a year or longer and they may have a quick trigger to anger as many believe the politicians have done them wrong. Do they have a legitimate beef to expect the politicians to put America first and stop sending their jobs overseas? The perception is brewing. And perception becomes reality. Many of the people who are out of work and have sacrificed see their politicians as "fat cats" as there doesn't appear to be any sacrifice by Senator Kerry of Massachusetts with his half-million dollar yacht and Senator Harry Reid of Nevada becoming a millionaire. These are two of the Senators who have supported Obama's plan to hire more federal government employees even though Obama's administration has already added 200,000 to the federal payroll.

On February 17, 2011 in Wisconsin the Governor, Scott Walker, is attempting to solve the state's deficit problem of $3 Billion Dollars. The state teachers receive an excellent salary, health care, and a huge pension. The teachers do not contribute any money to their pension fund. Almost all pension funds in the private sector require their employees to contribute money to their pension fund.

The Governor wants to pass a state law to have the teachers contribute 5.6% to their pension and 12% to their health care. The teachers are represented by a union. The teachers demonstrated on school days instead of being in the classroom teaching. A number of these teachers while on the scene of their demonstrations claimed they were sick in order to accept a doctor's permission to skip school. Is that fraud? Should there be consequences? Do you want your teachers to have a value system that dismisses their responsibility to teach the children and if they committed fraud to teach those values to your kids? The Wisconsin state Republican legislators want to solve their budget problem but so far the state Democratic legislators supported by the unions don't. These Democratic legislators disappeared to Illinois for a month instead of going to their job and voting on this and other issues. President

Obama said that elections have consequences. It appears elections only have consequences when the Democrats win and when they lose they don't show up as a quorum is needed to vote on a bill.

The state Democrats in Indiana took a page from Wisconsin and left their state for five weeks. Is this the way democracy is supposed to work? What example does this teach our children?

Does it say when you don't get your way you can and should run away from your problems?

Our union President, Barack Obama, quickly came out with a statement supporting the teachers union. Instead of providing leadership to solve our country's problems President Obama supports the teachers protesting and rioting. It's obvious his push for educating the children of our country takes a back seat to the unions.

This issue involving public employees who have joined a union and have received an above average employment benefits package for many years and now asked to give up some of these benefits is just the tip of the iceberg as it will spread across our country. It's already come to a head in Wisconsin, Indiana, New Jersey, Ohio, New York, and coming to California. All in all it may come to a head in the 45 out of our 50 states that are in the red.

The majority of the American people are fed up with the lack of responsibility and leadership from Barack Obama as he continues to push his social agenda and reckless spending. Obama's budget calls for a DEFICIT of $1.65 Trillion Dollars for FY 2012.

America's debt and deficit has soared well past $14 Trillion Dollars and the Democratic Party has ignored the American people's voice as the election of November 2010 mandated. The Republican Party is attempting to do the American people's mandate but the Democratic Party led by Obama, Harry Reid, Nancy Pelosi, Dick Durbin and Anthony Wiener have their own agenda of increasing

America's debt and deficit in what could be perceived as UNAMERICAN.

Senator Harry Reid arguably is the LEAST RESPECTED U. S. Senator in the last 60 years. Vice President Joe Biden is perceived to make unreliable comments but Reid has surpassed him with his driveling nonsense.

Representative Nancy Pelosi arguably is the LEAST RESPECTED representative in the history of the United States. Her comment of you have to pass the Obamacare bill to find out what is in it is normal unintelligible rambling from her.

Senator Dick Durbin blindly follows the liberal Democratic Party line. Durbin said on FOX NEWS on March 6, 2011 he would not vote for more than $10 Billion Dollar cuts in the discretionary budget. He proudly supports Obama's deficit budget for FY 2012 of $1.65 Trillion Dollar deficit. So he would cut less than 1%.

The Government Accountability Office reported they had identified $200 Billion

Dollars in duplication of services and waste. It appears that Durbin has no problem with the duplication of services and waste. Does he like spending your taxpayer money?

Representative Anthony Wiener appears to be a "hothead" who likes to do his Democratic Party's bidding. He appears on various news media outlets and acts like a bully.

Our country is at a crossroads of whether we survive or cause our own demise. These four, Reid, Pelosi, Durbin, and Wiener along with Barack Obama, are at the center of America stopping to reduce the enormous unsustainable debt and deficit. It's almost as if they want America to fail and it can easily be the perception.

America remember Barack Obama was rated as the MOST LIBERAL senator in the U.S. Senate. His theme of CHANGE was never challenged by the main street media as to what CHANGE he had planned. It is perceived by most Americans that the main street media has liberal leanings but even they have been surprised by how far left Obama and the Democratic Party can go. But yet these so called PROFESSIONALS rarely ask the right questions or are afraid of knowing as there may be consequences.

If you read the book DREAMS FROM MY FATHER, Barack Obama espouses his father's dreams of socialism and redistribution of wealth. That appears to be Obama's agenda as well. Many have questioned whether Obama has done what is right for America or followed his own agenda which is destructive to our capitalist system, our economic business system.

Dinesh D'Souza in his book, "The Roots of Obama's Rage" states "we are today living out the script for America and the world that was dreamt up not by Obama but by Obama's father. How do we know this? Because Obama says so himself. Reflect for a moment on the title of his book. It's not DREAMS OF MY FATHER but rather DREAMS FROM MY FATHER. In other words, Obama is not writing a book about his father's dreams; he is writing a book about the dreams that he got from his father".

"Think about what this means. The most powerful country in the world is being governed according to the dreams of a Luo tribesman of the 1950s – a polygamist who abandoned his wives, drank himself into stupors, and bounced around on two iron legs (after his real legs had to be amputated because of a car crash caused by drunk driving). This philandering, inebriated African socialist, who raged against the world for denying him the realization of his anti-colonial ambitious, is now setting the nation's agenda through the reincarnation of his dreams in his son.

The son is the one who is making it happen, but the son is, as he candidly admits, only living out his father's dream. The invisible father provides the inspiration, and the son dutifully gets the job done. America today is being governed by a ghost."

Dinesh D'Souza is a President of a college in the USA. He is a highly respected domestic policy analyst and research scholar.

You decide if Barack Obama has the best interests for the United States of America.

1. The USA imports almost 80% of the oil/gas we need. That cost us billions and billions of dollars. Approximately 70% of the oil/gas comes from the Middle East as reported by former President George W. Bush. These Middle East countries have gotten rich from our lack of developing our own oil/gas resources which remains in the ground. Barack Obama compounded our shortage of oil/gas by establishing a moratorium on any new deep sea drilling in the Gulf Coast from April 2010 to February 2011.

Obama also extended his moratorium to the east coast, west coast and Alaska. This affected a million people as they lost their ability to earn a living and in some cases lost their life savings.

2. President Obama and his majority Democratic Party sheep passed the health care law now commonly called Obamacare over the wishes of 70% of the American people.

Using "voodoo" math Obama claimed his health care law would save America money but non bias economists said you cannot count the same $500 Billion twice. Secretary of Health and Human Services Kathleen Sebelius finally admitted that was what was done. The health care law is presently in the courts as over half of the states are unhappy with it. And over 1000 corporations including the unions have already received a waiver from Obama's people from having to implement the law.

3. Obama wants to pass a law called "cap and trade" which could cause havoc with the energy industry. Obama has admitted that it would "sky rocket energy prices". Obama's push is for wind energy which has proven not to be reliable as it requires another base energy source to be dependable. America has 250 years of coal in the ground and coal is 97% cleaner today that it was 60 years ago.

4. The border states to Mexico have asked Obama for more help to secure the borders as violence has escalated and more Americans have been killed. In particular the states of

Arizona and Texas have pleaded for help but to no avail.

5. As states attempt to balance their budgets, which are mandatory by law and a concept the federal government doesn't adhere to, the public sector unions with their higher salaries and benefit packages have been protesting and rioting. Obama has spoken out in favor of the public sector unions. Obama has authorized the hiring of over 200,000 public sector employees in this first two years in office.

6. American's foreign policy is in disarray. President Obama quickly supported the overthrow of our largest ally in the Middle East, Egypt, but would not support the overthrow of our number one enemy in the Middle East, Iran. He has also encouraged the overthrow of other Middle East countries. The odds are that the Muslim Brotherhood which is dominated by the JIHAD movement will control the Middle East. Is Obama playing out the DREAMS FROM HIS FATHER in his foreign policy decisions?

7. President Obama released his 2012 FY budget with a deficit of $1.65 Trillion Dollars. He claims he will be saving $40 Billion Dollars. The $40 Billion Dollars is less that 1% of the deficit of over $14 Trillion Dollars. How do you save even as little as $40,000,000,000 out of a deficit $14,000,000,000,000 when your budget is $1,650,000,000,000 in the RED? So take $40 Billion Dollars out of $1.65 Trillion Dollars means the result would be a deficit of $1,610,000,000,000.

So at the end of FY 2012 the deficit would be $14,000,000,000,000 plus $1,610,000,000,000 or $15,610,000,000,000. Where is the savings?

If interest rates rise even a little, it may dramatically increase the deficit even more.

If anyone has the right to protest it should be the American people.

The American people have a right to protest against the President and the Democratic Party. President Obama and the Democratic Party by their actions DO NOT WANT TO REDUCE OUR DEBT AND DEFICIT TO ANY

DEGREE TO MAKE A DIFFERENCE.
It is time that we Americans demand that our
elected politicians do what is right for America
-- reduce our debt and deficit – otherwise we
will go bankrupt as a country and that leads to
our downfall. Every empire in the history of
the world fell from within because of their
debt and deficit.

Let the FACTS decide not your EMOTION
what side you are on.

If you are a member of a union do you want to
be a part of bringing down the United States of
America? Some of President Obama's closest
friends and advisors have called for violence
in the past so they are not above calling for it
again. Union member unless you are for
bringing down our country suggest you stand
up to your union leadership. Let them know
you love your country.

Let them know you love your way of life. Let
them know you love your free time, your
sports, your hobbies, and your family and
friends. All of that could change in an instant.
If the union leadership calls for protesting and

if it gets out of hand, which it may, will this start AMERICA'S SECOND CIVIL WAR? Once it is started it may spread like a brush fire or like a snowball rolling down a hill. It will be almost impossible to stop. And by the time it gets stopped it may have caused such chaos in our country that there will be devastation everywhere. Is that what you want?

Then we would be so vulnerable that we could be attacked by one of our potential enemies, namely the Muslim Brotherhood JIHAD, Communist Russia, or Communist China. They could wait until we destroy most of our assets and each other in a horrific civil war then all they would have to do is show up and take over. If you want to live under JIHAD and Shari law assuming they would let you live or under a Communist regime then you should move there now. Life would be completely different.

So Democratic Party member you decide if you want to take your chances under JIHAD rule or Communist rule. That is the alternative to democracy. Do you want your rulers to tell you what to do and when to do it or be killed? These rulers can be brutal. They won't take any excuses. There won't be a liberal court system to protect you. You may be sent to prison or just disappear.

No one will ask any questions. America has gotten too soft and once we have rulers dictating our life it will be hard. You won't have any money and you won't have your house. They probably will split up your family. Face reality now because if you survive the American civil war the rulers who conquer us will make life intolerable. They don't like us is an understatement.

SO CHOOSE CAREFULLY!

The politicians won't tell you this. Most politicians don't think beyond their next election. And politicians will sugarcoat this and not tell you what may happen. You either support the attempt to reduce our debt and deficit or the alternative may be the scenario just spelled out. You need to tell your elected politicians in Washington to reduce our debt and deficit now!

PLEASE READ THE FOLLOWING LETTER. IT'S THE AGENDA, THE GOAL, OF THE PROGRESSIVE MOVEMENT.

Dear American:

How would you like to make $5 a day for eight hours of work?

Impossible you say! The STANDARD OF LIVING in Kenya, Africa, Indonesia, India, China, and many other parts of the world is less than that. Yes, most workers in these countries make $2 or $3 dollars a day. That's for a full day of work.

Since we are Americans we will give everyone a raise to $5 dollars a day. Then $5 a day times 7 days a week equals $35 dollars a week. Then $35 dollars a week times 52 weeks equals $1820 a year. Again because we are generous everyone will receive a bonus so that they will make $2000 dollars a year.

President Barack Obama wants to redistribute the incomes of Americans to those less fortunate countries of the world. That was his father's dream and Barack Obama is carrying out his father's dream. THAT HAS BECOME HIS AGENDA! The sooner you realize this the quicker you can react to his agenda. Barack Obama is a PROGRESSIVE LIBERAL LIKE HIS FATHER WAS. THAT'S THE AGENDA OF THE PROGRESSIVE MOVEMENT WHICH DOMINATES THE DEMOCRATIC PARTY.

Also an official of the World Bank said, "the inequality in the world has to stop and we have to redistribute the wealth to the poorer countries".

How do you redistribute the wealth? You dismantle the American economy piece by piece. One, you increase the federal debt by unfavorable fiscal policies and tax policies for business. Two, you increase the hiring of public sector employees. This adds to the debt and produces nothing positive and increases the burden on the private sector who pays all the bills for the government. Three, you borrow more and more money from other countries which increases our debt. We now owe China $950 Billion Dollars, Japan $800 Billion Dollars and Great Britain $500 Billion Dollars to name just a *few countries. The interest on the loans will be equal to our annual economic output, GDP, in the next few years assuming the interest rate stays as low as it is today. Once the interest rate raises even just a little we are in deep trouble.*

Unless the American people wake up and stop this Progressive movement the average income of Americans in 25 years will be in the $20,000 Dollars a year range. Very few people will make above $20,000 Dollars a year.

When the American people voted in November 2010 they needed to vote for politicians who would stop this madness. They needed to vote for a Conservative. The American people woke up and voted in enough Conservatives in the House of Representatives but failed in their voting for the Senate Conservatives.

You think the riots in Europe and the Middle East are disturbing? YOU AIN'T SEEN NOTHING YET! Once Obama gets "Card Check" into law the labor unions have a free pass to unionize any company they want without a SECRET ballot. The union leaders are like the elected politicians they can focus on only one thing, that's more and more. This figures into the Obama plan as there will be more union members. They will not want to give up any of their wages and benefits. The companies will not be able to afford providing any more which results in all out clashes, riots as you have not seen before. Companies will either go out of business or go overseas to survive. The union workers will also have lost as there will not be any jobs. IT'S A NO WIN FOR ALL PARTIES INVOLVED EXCEPT THE PROGRESSIVE AGENDA. And this will happen throughout the country creating chaos everywhere.

A LITTLE KNOWN FACT IS THAT FDR, FRANKLIN D. ROOSEVELT, A DEMOCRAT, WAS TOTALLY AGAINST ANY UNION IN THE PUBLIC SECTOR. HE SAID HAVING A UNION IN THE PUBLIC SECTOR COULD BE CATASTROPHIC. FDR was the President of the United States of America from 1933 to 1945 longer than any person in our history. FDR is still the most popular Democratic Party President in USA history.

Once a family unit is in peril and they do not have the basics of life like food and shelter chaos is the result and it will be rampant.

It's a NOBLE thing to help the poor people in the

poorer nations in the world. America has given billions and billions of dollars to these countries for decades. Our money has done very little good as corruption has been and still is widespread in these countries. We need to find another more effective means of helping the poor. We need to do it without destroying America. We need to invoke the "fish story". That is we need to teach them to fish on their own without us always having to give them the fish.

A strange thing happened at the end of World War II. The victor not only defeated their enemy but also RESTORED them. What a novel idea! What a concept! So if we examine what happened then can we learn from that and come up with a practical strategy to ADVANCE the poorer nations of the world. The big difference of course was that Germany and Japan were an educated class, hard working, and industrious. But all things are possible if you only believe and commit to a purpose, a goal.

The first big problem is that we don't have any real leadership in this country. The leadership does not know what it takes to run a business or manage a country or create REAL POSITIVE CHANGE. All we have is a politician who gives speeches.

Many of the people around our leader are more into destroying something as opposed to building something positive.

Respectfully,
A VERY CONCERNED CITIZEN

If you know anything about American history you have probably heard about our Founding Fathers. Just mentioning a few of them may refresh your memory, people like George Washington, John Adams, Thomas Jefferson, Ben Franklin, James Madison, and Samuel Adams. These men along with all of those who were a part of the Continental Congress created our American Constitution. A Constitution which is as perfect today as it was when it was created. BUT OUR FOUNDING FATHERS MADE ONE MAJOR MISTAKE. THEY ASSUMED THAT THE PEOPLE THAT WOULD FOLLOW THEM WOULD LOVE OUR COUNTRY AS MUCH AS THEY DID. It was beyond their imagination that people following them one day would want to destroy the country they fought so hard to create. These Founding

Fathers risk their lives, their properties, their everything, to make it right. Today's congressman/congresswoman DOES NOT risk his/her life, property, or anything except for possibly not being reelected. It appears that the major concern of today's politician is to receive as much special interest money as possible to run all those television commercials to get reelected. The big problem is that special interest money has strings attached -- vote for and spend money for those special interests. In many, if not most instances, those votes do not represent the right thing to do for our country.

THE GLOBAL ECONOMY

A major factor that has produced the financial situation in our country that we are presently in is the GLOBAL ECONOMY.

First, our economic production has been drastically reduced. In 1960, 7 out of 10 workers were employed in manufacturing compared to only 2 out of 10 workers in 2010. America was known for being a manufacturing country. Today we are a service oriented country. For starters government employees outnumber private sector employees. Government employees do not manufacture anything, they have no product to sell. Second, for argument sake we will use 1980 for the starting point of the beginning of the mass exodus of American manufacturing corporations to China. Yes, we have also gone into several other countries namely South Korea, Mexico, India, and Ireland. Why did our manufacturing go overseas? Cheap labor resulting in huge corporate profits.

Simply, American labor unions wanted more and more and the management of these corporations did not want to stand up to the unions. It was easier to just go to China where the workers earned several dollars a day compared to over a hundred dollars a day then to fight the unions. Thus began the outsourcing of American jobs overseas and the layoff of millions of American workers, most of them union workers. Congress in its wisdom even provided incentives.

This is the beginning of the global economy. And it's the goal of some people in America for workers all over the world to earn the same as everyone else. Simply put, workers in China, India, South Korea, and Mexico, etc. should earn what American workers earn. Since workers in the world make considerably less than American workers their goal is to lower the incomes of American workers. It is time for the American people to wake up. And this includes all those government employees as the private sector shrinks even more there will not be enough left to pay their salaries and benefits. America is in a downward spiral unless we make an abrupt change in course.

What is the solution to this problem of sending American jobs overseas? First, the American people need to get involved and understand the reality of the global economy concept. Once they realize that they will be earning what the Chinese workers earn they may revolt. Even the workers in the unions may revolt once they understand this global economy concept. The union leaders have kept the union workers in line with promises that they cannot keep. Every American worker, union and non-union, will suffer the same fate. The union members are just being used by their leadership for the short term goal. President Obama has added 200,000 federal employees in his first two years in office. He knows that this adds millions of dollars to our deficit. His over the top spending is unsustainable and it may break our economy. Did Obama hire all these new federal employees to have an "army" of union members to combat the Americans who are trying to restore financial order to our country? Why are union members being transported all over the country to create chaos?

The Democratic Party is hopelessly lost. Most of the Democratic Party politicians don't even know that they are in the Progressive Party. It costs millions of dollars to start a new political party and it's better to camouflage the true intentions of the Progressive movement as most Democratic Party voters just vote the party line.

This is a built in starting point for millions of votes for the Progressives. The Democratic Party has done and is doing anything and everything it can for the labor unions.

The Republican Party is as much to blame for our mess as the Democratic Party. The Republican Party has done anything and everything in the name of business. Whatever business wants the Republican Party has attempted to do. There have been very few if any Republican politicians who have thought beyond a short term fix for the business solution. Providing incentives for American business to go overseas has come home to roost as they are as responsible for the global economy as anyone. Without knowing it they have provided the Progressive movement with the tools to reach their goals, of equal pay for everyone all over the world. It's like the British Commander in the World War II movie, "Bridge Over the River Kwai" who builds the bridge for the Japanese and at the last minute realizes what he has done and blows it up. He had that "aha" moment but will the Republicans?

So the solution is painful but to continue the status quo is absolutely the downfall of capitalism, the downfall of our economy. To continue will eventually lead to everyone in the world earning the same. We will be like the "third world countries" and they will be like us. There will be no more American "exceptionalism". We need to stop the nonsense now!

We need to reverse our laws allowing American corporations to send jobs overseas. No more incentives to do so. Next we need to put a heavy tax on any American corporation that imports their products from overseas. Also, as many countries don't have a level playing field in regard to imports and exports with the USA, we need to add an import tax for those countries that require a tax on our products. These actions will not be popular but we need to be in a survival mode. These actions should generate more manufacturing jobs in the USA. Also, it appears that almost everything you buy at Wal Mart has the "Made in China" label on it. The quality of many of the products is not up to American standards.

We need a commitment from the labor unions to re-negotiate their contracts to insure that American corporations will have an equal playing field with foreign competition. Without the commitment corporations will lose and labor unions will lose. This will become the great debate in our country as the union leaders and the union members will have to agree to give up some of the wages and benefits that they bargained for. Management will have to stand up and negotiate real cuts and more than likely take a strike.

Management must be ready for whatever

comes which may include violence. The labor unions need to face reality that if they do not agree to cuts in their wages and benefits their employment in their manufacturing facility or their work place will be either drastically reduced or closed and all may be laid off. Union members must ask themselves do they want to work for reasonable pay and benefits or lose their job forever with their employer. This includes the union member standing up to their union bosses. The global economy is for real. It's now a global market place. Union worker China's economy is booming at your expense! Union worker India's economy is booming at your expense! The people of China and India are happy to have the jobs that you decided you did not want anymore. Because you gave them up they have a job. And China has a BILLION, 1,000,000,000, more people than the USA which translates into a lot of Chinese still willing to work.

Are you going to give them your job or will you face reality? Remember it's your Democratic President Barack Obama who wants to transform America and redistribute your job to China, India, and other countries so they can earn a decent living which will come at your expense. Union workers today have more education and on the whole are more educated than any time in our history. Union worker membership used to be around 50% of the private sector workforce but today it's only 7%. You are smart enough to understand why that is.

Union worker, not only are you competing with the global economy but also the industrial automation. Manufacturing plants today are highly automated. Many if not most high intensive labor jobs have been replaced by computers and automation. Union worker you can protect your job by wisely negotiating and agreeing to the reality of 2011. You cannot continue to live in the 1930s.

Union worker, management today is weaker as it relates to fighting a union or standing up to take a strike therefore they will agree to almost anything knowing that if and when their financial situation turns bad they will close the plant or work place and everyone will be laid off. So you need to think about what you are demanding as when your demands become intolerable you are looking for a new job. And good luck with finding a job as good as what you now have.

FREE TRADE?

The USA has many trade agreements with other countries. Most are considered "free trade agreements". In reality only a few are actually free trade agreements. In a highly volatile political country like the USA, a President and the U. S. Congress wants to show the American people that the potential for more jobs are in the future by publicizing a trade agreement which they have negotiated. The American people rarely see the details. Headlines are deceiving. In many, if not most, of these "free trade agreements" we ended up with the short end of the stick. Those future jobs Americans were promised more than likely ended up with the other country.

After World War II America was the industrial giant of the world.

Students of history will remember the names of the giants who developed our industries in the late 1800s and early 1900s, people like

Andrew Carnegie (steel), Henry Ford, Alfred Sloan, and Walter Chrysler (automobiles), Thomas Edison (consumer electronics), Robert Fulton (shipping), Orville and Wilbur Wright (airplanes), Eli Whitney (machine tools), and John D. Rockefeller (oil). We were the envy of the world. American factories were the envy of the world. We worked at "making things". We won World War II because of our ability to make the weapons systems needed to win.

Since World War II we have either given away our edge or had it copied. Our World War II enemies quickly became our friends as we helped to build up their economies. And then Germany and Japan became our main industrial competitors. How could these two small countries "invade and capitalize" on our industrial monopoly? Because we allowed it to happen. How?

One example, we "negotiated" a trade agreement with Japan. The agreement calls for Japan to have free access to all of our markets.

They quickly built things, cars which gained

25% of our market share, electronics, cameras, and steel products. But this trade agreement did not allow us free access to their markets. Yes, the country that attacked us and that we defeated when we had the power and authority allowed them through negotiations to close some of their markets to us. The result became a negative for the USA as our corporations couldn't compete and American job losses mounted up.

We signed a trade agreement with Mexico. Soon thereafter American corporations built manufacturing plants in Mexico to take advantage of the cheaper labor costs. The result became a negative for the USA as Americans lost their jobs.

We also have a trade agreement with India but we don't have equal access to their enormous market of one billion people. The result became a negative for the USA as American corporations went to India and Americans lost their jobs.

Former President Richard Nixon and Secretary of State Henry Kissinger opened up

Communist China to American and world trade in 1971. The philosophy was it's better to have some idea what they are doing as they are the most populated country in the world at one billion 300 million people. The reader may remember that this was during the Vietnam War and Communist China backed the North. Realists say that the North Vietnamese beat the South Vietnamese. Of further interest to our leaders at that time they wanted to know more about Communist China's military capabilities. Communist China exploded their first atomic bomb in 1964.

The result of the trade agreement with Communist China has been catastrophic for the American workers. Starting in 1980 American corporations were building manufacturing plants there at an alarming rate. American manufacturing corporations have built Communist China's economy where today it is the second largest industrial economy in the world overtaking the Japanese.

Meanwhile American workers have lost

millions of jobs. We don't have equal access to their markets. In 2011 China's economy is booming at around 10% growth while the American economy is fluttering at approximately 2%. Our U.S. Congress even provided incentives for our corporations to build overseas.

How smart was that? Well if you were a CEO of an American corporation that went overseas who made a ton of money your Board of Directors gave you a BIG bonus. American CEOs created the global economy.

REDUCING OUR FEDERAL DEFICITS BY REDUCING FEDERAL PROGRAMS AND DUPLICATION OF SERVICES

Let's reduce our national debt which will result in a reduction in our national deficit. Let's do something that has an IMMEDIATE IMPACT. Government employment is over 50% of the work force. We need to cut our federal payroll and all of those expensive benefits that government employees are receiving.

Federal pensions are mounting up and they are unfunded. It's a dumb idea to pay their high salaries and allow them to retire at 55 with half of their salaries or higher. No we don't need to pay them the high salaries to attract them to do government work. That's absurd!

First, a number of people have recommended

eliminating the Department of Education. The record shows the more money that is given to the Department of Education the education of America's children seems to drop. National test scores have steadily dropped for many years. One report said the public high school graduation rate is around 50%. In comparison the Catholic high school graduation rate is 97% and they don't receive any federal money. What has happened to the BILLIONS OF DOLLARS that the public schools have received?

This author's suggestion is to eliminate half of the Department of Education employees. The half that is remaining will be given five years to improve education across the country. If the education of America's children does not improve in those five years the Department of Education will be eliminated. If that were to happen education will be financed by giving the federal money required directly to the states on a per pupil basis. Each state will be receiving the same amount per pupil. Eliminating half of the employees of the Department of Education will save America millions and in time probably billions of dollars.

The Department of Education will still have enough money to create the three programs that the author is recommending. The author is suggesting three new programs and the importance of these new programs is that they will work plus have a positive impact on the individuals and their educational experience. Students in the 10th, 11th, and 12th grades are vulnerable and these educational programs may make a positive difference in their lives.

1. We could identify students who are struggling or on the verge of dropping out of school. We would provide a new environment one that stresses practical every day skills that could motivate the students away from just learning to pass a test. This could be more "a hands on" one on one educational experience. The curriculum could consist of more technical teachings.

A number of rural areas in our country are losing population and have been for decades. It's time to rethink our educational and training programs. Instead of the majority of programs centered in our larger population centers it could resolve the problem of reviving what could be described as near "ghost towns". Our depleted rural areas could house some of these educational programs. We could establish ten educational centers in rural areas around the country. Picture an educational campus where the students could live and learn skills which would give them 21st century abilities in our ever evolving world. This would be realistic learning skills which would qualify the participants for jobs. By taking the students out of their normal big city life and all the distractions and peer group pressures the students may have a NEW POSITIVE START. This would also create new jobs as buildings would need to be built to create the new educational campus.

2. We could develop science and math schools. We could identify students in the tenth grade who have an interest and aptitude in science and math and offer them a more challenging opportunity that a normal school system may not be able to offer. These students would spend their 11th and 12th

grades in a rural environment suitable for meeting the challenges. The environment would be away from many of the distractions experienced by most students in big cities.

The author's own experiences of living in a dormitory allowed him and the other students to learn independence and maturity of making decisions. The author suggests establishing a community for learning. Ideally building this community in a rural area with schools, dormitories, dining areas, administrators and master teachers could create inspiration for learning and individual development. Students and teachers could get together for "brainstorming sessions" which in time may create new ideas that could add to new discoveries in the sciences and math.

3. We could develop student health centers. We could identify students in the 10th grade who are overweight. These students may be overweight because of their environment. By putting them into a new environment focused on developing healthy bodies and positive attitudes and habits. This may prevent a whole range of health problems. This not only

will provide a healthy lifestyle it may save millions of dollars in future health care costs.

Again we would provide this environment in a rural area. The students would live in dormitories for their 11th and 12th grades. The focus would be on physical activities as well as other educational subjects. This would provide opportunities for health care providers, nutritionists, physical conditioning professionals, and other teachers.

Second, President Obama has already added over 200,000 federal employees in his first two years in office. The Government Accountability Office, GAO, reported during the last week of February 2011 that DUPLICATION OF PROGRAMS AND WASTE COST THE TAXPAYERS $200 BILLION DOLLARS.

Therefore all of the federal departments except for national defense/national security will lay off 10% of their employees 60 days after the passage of this law. An additional 5% will be laid off from these same departments in another 60 days or 120 days from the passage of this law. This will SAVE millions of dollars and in time probably billions.

Third, in the Department of Defense there are over 20,000 contractors working for the federal government and employed in Afghanistan and Iraq. Are there REALLY 20,000 different functions to be performed in Afghanistan and Iraq? Does the Secretary of Defense Robert Gates have any idea what all of these contractors are doing? How many employees are employed by these 20,000 contractors? How much DUPLICATION is going on? Can it be assumed that these employees are earning a much higher pay than if they were a part of our military. How much CONTROL and OVERSIGHT is there over these 20,000 contractors? How does one COORDINATE with 20,000 contractors? And how much COORDINATION is there among the 20,000 contractors and in reality how much should there be? I think the reader gets the point. Couldn't some of these jobs be performed by our military personnel at a much lower cost to our federal government?

Our tax policy is broken. We need to make adjustments to it. The author looked at the "flat tax" proposals and none in his opinion are equitable to individual people or the corporations. There needs to be allowable deductions because of the diverse industries many of which require an exception to not only stay in business but to make even a small profit. That's why our present tax code is thousands of pages. Individuals also need some deductions such as for mortgage(s), health insurance premiums, investor dividends/capital gains, child care, to name some.

The author spoke to an experienced certified public accountant, (CPA) in reference to the corporate exemptions. Many who favor a "flat tax" also favor deleting all the corporate exemptions.

The CPA said that if the exemptions were deleted the lobbyists would be successful in having almost all of them reinstated within two years. So instead of Congress spending years of going through each paragraph of each section and debating the value of each and then haggling and playing politics a simple solution is to keep it as is.

One of the problems associated with the tax system is that many large corporations earn billions of dollars and pay no tax, zero. The author has heard many television business commentators report that as many as two thirds of the large corporations don't pay any federal income tax. The American people hearing this from time to time get upset because they pay tax on what little they make and these corporations get off scot-free.

President Obama and the Democrats have continually gone after the super rich those in the top 2% in our country. They have wanted to tax them at a higher rate which is logical. When one considers that the top 400 families own approximately 50% of the wealth in the USA and they pay on average only 16% federal income tax something should be done. Bill Gates, the Microsoft founder, has said that his secretary pays a higher percentage then he does. Most middle class Americans pay a higher percentage than the super rich. It is believed that the majority of Americans believe in capitalism. The majority of Americans also believe that the super rich and the other multi-millionaires should pay their fair share. It is time to require the wealthy to contribute their fair share.

The SIXTY MINUTES television show on March 27, 2011 presented a segment on corporations avoiding paying federal income tax. The reporter, Lesley Stahl, stated that hundreds of American corporations have moved their corporate headquarters overseas especially to Switzerland. The author has been to Switzerland and considers it one of the most beautiful countries in the world. But that isn't the reason these tax avoiding corporations have gone there. Switzerland has one of the lowest income tax rates in the world at 16%. There are other countries with lower income tax rates than the USA and our corporations are also there.

 The problem besides moving overseas is that these American corporations ONLY moved overseas ON PAPER WITH A LEGAL FILING BUT THEY DID NOT MOVE THEIR

CORPORATE HEADQUARTERS STAFF INCLUDING THE CEO AND CFO. Only a few after publicity have gotten out has transferred their CEO and CFO overseas. Lesley Stahl stated that American corporations have approximately $2 TRILLION DOLLARS overseas that is not in the reach of the IRS. American corporations claim they cannot compete in the global market.

But you be the judge. American corporations are having record profits. They have $2 Trillion Dollars in cash in their bank accounts in the USA and $2 Trillion Dollars overseas. They have numerous write offs in their businesses and over half or two thirds don't pay any federal income tax. And those that do pay any federal income tax pay at a lower rate than the 35% rate listed by the IRS. It appears that greed is the driving force of these CEOs.

The more profit they can show the bigger their salaries and bonuses which could be in the millions. The figures don't lie.

American corporations are competing

extremely well in this global economy!

Let's stop the madness! Corporations that want to go overseas to avoid paying federal income taxes should face stiff penalties.

Why? 'It's like having your cake and eating it to." Because they laid off Americans in the USA to manufacture their products overseas. Americans cannot afford the corporations doing this.

We can either ban their products from coming in the USA or have them pay a tax. Since they are avoiding paying income tax then we can impose an import tax on their products. There should not be a free lunch for these corporations. There is no free lunch for the average American citizen. The author suggests a tax of 40% on any product coming into the USA. This helps to offset for some of the cheap labor overseas. The corporation needs to declare the product(s), the volume, and the value of their cargo at the port of entry. They will be required to deliver a corporate check to the U.S. Treasury for the 40% of the value of their cargo. If American corporations don't want to import anymore than that opens up a void that can be filled by new American corporations. This will be controversial but it may stop the mass exodus of our American jobs from going overseas. This import tax will apply to all American corporations and any of their subsidiaries that are overseas including those that have been overseas for thirty years.

IT'S TIME AMERICAN CORPORATIONS HIRED AMERICANS IN AMERICA!

PROPOSED FEDERAL INCOME TAX FOR AMERICAN CORPORATIONS AND ANY FOREIGN CORPORATION DOING BUSINESS IN THE USA

The federal income tax for American corporations and any foreign corporation doing business in the USA will be 25%.

Corporations will keep their exemptions as stated in the IRS code.

For corporations earning over $5 Million Dollars a year there will be a "pre-tax" of 1% on gross earnings. The "pre-tax" will be paid at a rate of one quarter of 1% per quarter. This will require all large corporations to at least pay some federal income tax. This will stop these large corporations from not paying any federal income taxes. This will be a new federal revenue source and may add up to billions of dollars for any given year which will go directly to the federal government treasury account. These tax receipts/monies by law should be obligated to go directly to reducing our national deficit.

PROPOSED FEDERAL INCOME TAX RATES FOR INDIVIDUALS

This is the proposed federal income tax for American individuals working in the USA and those working overseas. This eliminates some of the tax breaks for Americans working overseas. Individuals will keep their exemptions as stated in the IRS code except for the overseas exemption. The exemptions for the rich won't change as their federal income tax will be based on their gross earnings.

THE FOLLOWING RATE
SCHEDULE WILL APPLY

Earning less than	20,000	no tax
Earning	20,001 to 40,000	8% NET
Earning	40,001 to 80,000	10% NET
Earning	80,001to 120,000	13% NET
Earning	120,001to 200,000	15% NET
Earning	200,001to 350,000	19% NET
Earning	350,001to 500,000	23% NET
Earning	500,001to 1 million	28% NET
Earning	1 million +1 to 2 million	33% NET
Earning	2 million +1 to 5 million	5% of GROSS
Earning	over 5 million	7% of GROSS

PRESIDENT OBAMA'S BUDGET
FOR 2012
TOTAL $3.73 TRILLION –
$3,730,000,000,000

PROJECTED REVENUES – $2.20 TRILLION
PROJECTED EXPENSES -- $3.85 TRILLION
PROJECTED DEFICIT   -- $1.65 TRILLION

DEPARTMENT BUDGETS
Dollar amounts are in the Billions of Dollars

DEPT BUDGETED SAVINGS

Agriculture	$144,014	$29 Billion
Commerce	13,142	1.3
	SEE FOOTNOTE	
Defense	707,467	0
Education	70,467	35
	SEE FOOTNOTE	
Energy	43,089	21.5
	SEE FOOTNOTE	

Health & Human Services	892,811	84
Homeland Security	46,913	4.6
Housing & Urban Development	49,399	7.3
Interior	13,912	2
Justice	33,151	5
Labor	109,026	16
State	62,609	6
Transportation	89,622	20
Infrastructure spending	556	100
Plus another	128	?
Treasury	114,507	17
Veteran Affairs	124,332	0
EPA	9,986	5,486
SEE FOOTNOTE		
NASA	18,174	1.8
SBA	1,205	0

FOOTNOTE: move DEPT of EPA, DEPT of SBA, and DEPT of ENERGY to DEPT of COMMERCE. DEPT of EDUCATION on 5 year probation. If no improvement in students test scores move to DEPT of COMMERCE and evaluate further.

NEW PROPOSED
DEPARTMENT BUDGETS

Agriculture	$115,014
Commerce	11,842 + 4.5 + 1.2 + 21.5 = 39,844
Defense	707,467
Education	35,927
Health & Human Services	42,099
Interior	11,912
Justice	28,151
Labor	93,026
State	56,609
Transportation	69,622
Infrastructure	456,000 +128
Treasury	97,507
Veteran Affairs	124,332
NASA	16,374

Total cuts -- $355 Billion Dollars – This figure includes the federal employees to be laid off as explained in the DEFICIT REDUCTION SECTION. Remember we cut 10% of the federal workforce in 60 days and then another

5% in 120 days.

Remember the GAO identified $200 Billion Dollars in duplication services and waste.

Since Barack Obama became President the federal government has added over 200,000 new federal employees.

NEW REVENUE SOURCES will add approximately $1 Trillion Dollars in income for the first year which goes to reduce the deficit.

Savings/deductions -- cut federal civil service salaries by 10% then freeze salaries for two years. Have federal civil service employees contribute a minimum of 15% toward their health care and 15% toward their pension. Reduce pension to no more than 25% of monthly salary. Require federal workers to retire at the same age as people in the private sector at age 65. Federal employees are not any better than other Americans.

Bowles and Simpson suggested cutting congressional and white house budgets by 15% and eliminate 20,000 contractors out of 250,000 non-defense service and staff augmentee contractors saving $18.4 Billion Dollars.

Example of some duplication in the federal budget:
  1. 47 job training programs
  2. 56 programs teaching financial literacy
  3. 15 agencies doing food safety
  4. 82 teacher training quality programs -- yet student test scores get worse and dropout rates rise

---

It is time we stop the madness of electing Presidents who want to spend more money than our revenues. It is time that we elected our next five Presidents from universities other than Harvard, Yale, and Columbia.

DEFICIT REDUCTION BY ADDING NEW REVENUE SOURCES

It is time to get serious about DEFICIT REDUCTION. Most Americans understand that as our deficits grow our American way of life will become unsustainable. We either destroy ourselves with the heavy debt and deficit or we pick ourselves up and fight this virus that has entered our body politic.

We must find an acceptable balance between income and spending.

The following are some examples of income that are well overdue.

First, many reports over the years have stated that two-thirds of the large corporations in our country DO NOT pay any federal income taxes. The CEO, chief executive officer, of a corporation can decide whether to pay federal income taxes or put money into a business venture. This is usually an easy decision for the CEO as greed is a wonderful thing and the more profits he can show will put another feather in his cap. It is time for these corporations to pay some federal income taxes. These corporations can report billions or millions of dollars profit without paying any federal income taxes. For the most part it is and has been the Republican Party that has protected BIG business. Now Republican Party it is time you got your act together as these unfair business practices need to stop. Those who benefit the most need to pay their fair share.

Since the corporations don't want to pay any federal income tax based on their NET TAX we therefore need to pass a CORPORATE GROSS TAX. A gross tax per quarter is needed.

So let's tax the corporations ONE-QUARTER OF ONE PERCENT per quarter. That would equal to one percent per year.

This should generate revenues of a minimum of $500 BILLION DOLLARS PER YEAR. These revenues should go directly into paying down the deficit.

Second, we need to pass a PENALTY TAX on the Wall Street corporations who caused the financial meltdown problems. Any corporation that received a bailout in the financial fiasco should be held responsible. Some of these Wall Street corporations are ALREADY paying millions of dollars in bonuses as if nothing happened. While millions of Americans have been affected by the madness of these Wall Street executives the madness has returned.

Millions of Americans have lost much and may never recover by the acts of these madmen. WALL STREET'S INTER-PRETATION OF THE GOLDEN RULE NEEDS TO CHANGE. THEIR BELIEF IS "WHOEVER HAS THE GOLD, RULES" IS NOT ACCEPTABLE ANYMORE.

Therefore, on top of the corporate gross tax a penalty tax of one-half of one percent per quarter is added for causing the financial pain. This will equal to 2% per year. This tax may be called "the American pain tax." This should generate a minimum of several hundred billion dollars a year. These revenues will go directly to pay down the deficit.

In addition a thorough investigation should be conducted into the wisdom of mingling bad assets with sound assets and selling them in investment packages where the buyer needs to be made aware of their real risks. There needs to be corporate integrity in offering a product to the market that has actual value and is backed by a real asset. We need to stop the legislative influence of those who have received special interest money. For example, that which lowered the standards of buying a house, and subsequently receiving campaign contributions from such interests groups should be forbidden. As members of the U. S. Congress are immune to punishment for their legislative actions EVERY GOVERNOR MUST INITIATE A LAW TO REMOVE THIS IMMUNITY OF MEMBERS OF CONGRESS SO THEY CAN BE HELD ACCOUNTABLE FOR THEIR ACTIONS, AND THEREFORE PROPERLY PROSECUTED TO THE FULLEST EXTENT OF THE LAW. It is highly unlikely that this law would pass the U. S. Congress therefore the Governors must act to have an amendment eliminating immunity for members of the U. S. Congress. It is high time that we restore honesty and integrity in the U.S. Congress.

Third, is the elimination of corporate incentives to export jobs overseas. This is mentioned in another section of the book. This will result in adding billions of dollars and will go directly in paying down the deficit.

Fourth, is an import tax on American corporations that manufacture products overseas and bring them into the USA, thereby having eliminated American jobs. This is mentioned and explained in another section of the book. This should add revenue to our treasury but is difficult to measure.

Fifth, is to establish a level playing field for all of our trading partners. This is a FAIR TAX with all the countries that have a tax or tariff on American products going into their countries. At whatever rate our products are taxed we will institute the same rate on products entering the USA. As the USA has the largest economy in the world we should not have to pay a tax to any country. Every

foreign corporation or foreign country
wanting to sell their products to our
prosperous economy must be charged an
import tax as long as that country charges us.
It is regrettable, but if we open our markets
they need to open theirs. This should add
to our treasury but again is difficult to
measure.

Sixth, is the United States Postal Service. The
post office is losing millions of dollars every
year. It will save millions of dollars
annually by having a FIVE DAY DELIVERY
OF MAIL A WEEK. U.S. CONGRESS GET
OVER IT AND GET IT DONE.

Seventh, it is time that we did more than just
talk in empty rhetoric to the people who allow
99% of the rest of the Americans to live the
American lifestyle. YES veterans allow 99% of
the rest of the population to live the American
lifestyle. It is time to respect the occupation of
the military. For those who have sacrificed so
much it is time that we give them some of the
pie. Every veteran who retires with twenty
years of active military service receives a
military pension. That pension needs to be

increased. For the veterans who fall short of the twenty years of active military service there should be an appreciation of the years they served our country. The author proposes that once a veteran reaches 65 he will be allowed to draw his full SOCIAL SECURITY monthly payment regardless of any statues to the contrary. To honor the service of the veteran a 2% increase per year of active duty service should be added to his normal Social Security monthly payment.

This will become an incentive for the veteran to stay on active duty status for a longer period of time. The result of this will benefit the country by having more veterans stay longer providing for a more stable national defense.

Eighth, is the author's proposal for Social Security. The full retirement age is raised to 67 ½ to receive the full retirement pay.

For individuals needing to retire at 63 they will receive 60% of their full retirement pay. There will be no ceiling on the earnings of an individual subject to the Social Security tax. Currently this is limited to the first $106,800. The old saying, "to whom much is given much is required" has NOT been a fact of life. To the "fortunate" among us it will become a fact. The maximum monthly Social Security payment will be capped at $3000 Dollars.

These adjustments will generate enough revenues to keep the Social Security system solvent for many years.

Ninth, the Capital Gains rate is to be 20%.

Tenth, according to Mr. Bowles and Mr. Simpson the sale of unused federal properties will net $8 Billion Dollars.

CAN AMERICA RELY ON A TRANSPORTATION SYSTEM THAT IS AT THE MERCY OF THE EVER INCREASING FOREIGN OIL/GAS?

April 2010 we had the BP oil spill. President Obama took his time in going to the Gulf Coast to provide leadership. But it didn't take him too much time in establishing a MORATORIUM ON ALL DEEP SEA DRILLING IN THE GULF. THEN ON FEBRUARY 28, 2011 HE AUTHORIZED THE FIRST DEEP SEA DRILLING PERMIT. THAT WAS 314 DAYS FROM THE OIL SPILL.

MILLIONS OF PEOPLE IN THE GULF REGION LOST THEIR JOBS AND LIVELIHOODS BECAUSE OF THE LONG DELAY.

If an airplane were to crash on President Obama's time in office would he ground all airplanes for 314 days? That's a reasonable question to ask.

We need a real stimulus project that will have merit and create millions of well paying jobs. Former President Dwight Eisenhower saw how effective the German "autobahn" was and he created our national highway system of freeways from coast to coast. Also, the Germans and most European countries have a passenger railroad system which is very effective and allows their peoples to travel wherever they want. The side benefit of the passenger railroad system is that the train gets 420 miles to the gallon. Most passenger cars today are lucky if they get 30 miles to the gallon. A recent Government Accountability Office, (GAO), news report said that we use 85 million gallons of gas a day in our country. Every twelve days the USA uses one billion barrels of oil. The USA uses 25% of the world's oil but only produces 2% of it. In 1980 the world oil production peaked and since then the oil production has been reduced 2% per year. If you are thinking ahead BP, Shell, and Exxon have only 2% of the world's oil reserves. On the other hand Saudi Arabia and Russia have the most oil reserves. The fast growing economies of Communist China and India import almost 100% of their oil. The report further stated that beginning in 30 years oil production may become scarce. The logical conclusion is that the price of oil and gas will sky rocket as early as five years from now. Five dollars a gallon for gas is a real possibility. Thirty years from now gas may easily be $10 a gallon.

Another factor in favoring passenger train service is that our current forms of transportation, roads and airports, are close to capacity in what they can handle. Reports have estimated that several TRILLIONS of dollars are needed to correct the problems associated with roads and airports. Also, 30 years from now our population growth could add another 100 million people on our existing infrastructure. This could result in a nightmarish situation.

Building more roads and airports would be very expensive and would require more dependence on oil/gas. Also, creating a transportation system based on utilizing busses would be dependent on oil/gas.

Most of our elected politicians rarely think

beyond their next election. This is short sightedness. There is very little long range planning. Most Americans will be hard pressed to purchase enough gas for all of their needs when the price of gas sky rockets.

The transportation of people and goods are dependent on oil/gas.

For many years our elected officials from both political parties have given away billions of dollars to foreign countries to help develop their economies and infrastructure. Those countries which didn't have widespread corruption used that money effectively.

Many developed transportation systems especially railroads and passenger train services. Thirty years from now when oil/gas is scarce or too expensive how will Americans get around? The populated areas in our country like New York City, Boston, Chicago, and Los Angeles have an abundance of passenger train services but what about the 200 million American people who don't? If we had a passenger train system from coast to coast we could save millions of dollars in gas daily. This would greatly cut our dependence on foreign oil/gas. Are the people in New York City, Boston, Chicago, and Los Angeles any better than the people in the Midwest or southwest? Don't think so! These people and wherever there is a passenger train service have had the convenience of travel that trains provide. There are over a thousand trains that go into Grand Central Station in New York City every day!

It is time to build a first rate passenger train system all over the country so that all Americans can benefit. Most people who travel from New York City going west and travel across our great country for the first time are amazed at the vastness and beauty.

Once they pass through Ohio, Kansas, Colorado, Wyoming, and Texas they will see the beauty and vastness. It becomes obvious the distances between the cities. Our aging population could ride in comfort as they sit back and enjoy the scenery. My recommend-action would be trains that travel up to 90 miles an hour.

Some people who think of trains want them to speed at 150 to 200 miles an hour which in my thinking is unsafe and creates stress in the passengers. It is not easy to relax at 200 miles an hour even if you are not driving. This building of a railroad passenger system would be a massive project and would create millions of well paying jobs. The proposed railroad system could be divided into several projects geographically and the railroad corporations could bid similar to defense contracts. But these would be loans to these corporations. The corporations can repay the loans from the fees they charge the passengers. A thought to those who say look at Amtrak they are losing money every year even though they have enough ridership. Amtrak is run by the federal government. It could be more efficient and also raise their low prices to a more realistic price structure and therefore show a profit. With a thousand trains going into Grand Central Station in New York City every day there should be profits. If not than they need to reduce the number of trains going into there.

Thirty years from now the American people are going to ask why didn't we build a passenger train service as they won't be able to afford the high prices of gas to get to work or buy food, or etc.

Reality is now as oil/gas will be scarce. Let's plan ahead.

OUR MILITARY

The author doesn't see the members of the U.S. Congress being patriotic enough to quit their jobs, join the military, and go fight in the war. Of the original group of men and women who went to Iraq and then Afghanistan to fight in the wars almost half have been killed or injured. They were required to go back into the wars four or five tours of at least a year each. It's a great relief when they returned home from a tour in the war zone especially unscathed only to return again to the war zone in a year. This rotation has continued four or five times for our combat troops.

The problem is we only have one and a half million active duty military personnel and they are divided into the Army, Air Force, Navy, Marines, and Coast Guard. The Army has approximately 550,000 military personnel and of that number ONLY HALF are combat troops. Are you thinking what I am thinking?

Yes, we need to increase our active duty military. In 1960 the USA had two million active duty military personnel when our population was 150 million people. In 2011 we have 308 million people but 25% less active duty military personnel. Is there any American above a third grade education who doesn't think this is absurdity?

Can you imagine for a moment being married and having a family.

Then you have to leave your family every other year for a whole year and you have to do this for eight or ten years. Married life and family life can be rough enough without being apart every other year for up to ten years. Divorce rates are around 50% and that's in non-military families. Therefore many military families may not have a stable marriage or family life. The result is there are too many suicides among the spouse who has come home from the war and finds himself in an emotional state with the family life.

No wonder there are so many suicides!

During the House Armed Services Committee meeting during the first week of April 2011 which was televised on C-SPAN, four star General Duncan McNabb the Commander of the US Transportation Command made some very alarming statements.

The Congresswoman from Hawaii asked about the makeup of his command who were assisting with supplying the war zones.

McNabb stated that 60% of his personnel were National Guard and Reservists and 40% were active duty military personnel. He also stated that his military transportation command uses a tremendous amount of commercial/civilian aircraft to get the job done. THIS IS ALARMING AS WE EITHER DO NOT HAVE ENOUGH ACTIVE DUTY MILITARY PERSONNEL TO GET THE JOB DONE AND WE DO NOT HAVE ENOUGH MILITARY AIRCRAFT TO GET THE JOB DONE.

It is disturbing that we need to require our National Guard units from the various states to go overseas and perform duties that should be done by our active duty military personnel. Our National Guard units were designed to remain in the USA and perform their tasks within our country. The state National Guard units are our last defense against anything that may happen to us and if they are overseas then they won't be able to defend us.

Secretary of Defense Robert Gates has said that he is using 20,000 contractors in the Afghanistan war.

WHAT IS THE MAKEUP OF OUR MILITARY DEFENSE?

ARE WE RELYING TOO MUCH ON GUARDSMEN WHO HAVE OTHER FULL TIME JOBS AND ARE REQUIRED FROM TIME TO TIME TO DO NATIONAL DEFENSE WORK?

ARE WE RELYING ON CIVILIAN CONTRACTORS TO DO NATIONAL DEFENSE WORK? ARE WE RELYING TOO MUCH ON SEVERAL HUNDRED THOUSAND MILITARY COMBAT TROOPS

WHO HAVE BEEN AT WAR FOR TEN
YEARS? If you went beyond the third grade
you know the answer! YES! YES! YES!

Yes, we need to increase our active duty
military. How many combat troops would we
need if we had to fight Communist China
or Russia or both? There is a good chance we
will one day! Why?

Remember the goal of the Communist
philosophy is they want to take over the
world. Also, the Muslim JIHAD wants to take
over the world. Since our "heroes" in the U. S.
Congress won't fight in the war they should
make it more tolerable for our "true heroes"
who are. This would increase our military
defense and national defense. Also, this could
generate millions of more jobs as we would
need to re-open some of those bases we closed
ten years ago. In my opinion we can cut other
programs to reduce the deficit but we need a
strong defense now.

If we add up the people hired for the
passenger train/railroad system and the re-
opening of military bases and the additional

active duty military personnel we probably have a total of five to seven million new jobs. This adds up to a robust economy! And if you add the fact that American corporations will be doing more manufacturing within the USA this may add millions of new jobs. Add all of this together we could be in for decades of prosperity!

THE NEW START TREATY

Surprise! Surprise! All of a sudden the
Communist Chinese have a "stealth bomber"
and a missile that can destroy an "aircraft
carrier" without anyone in the Defense
Department having had any prior knowledge.
Secretary of Defense Robert Gates has spent
his time on such topics as eliminating our
missile defense system for Poland and the
Czech Republic, eliminating a new bomber
program, don't ask don't tell, the START
treaty with Russia, and not deciding on an
aircraft refueling tanker that is ten years
behind schedule which was just approved in
2011. Does this show Mr. Gates is strong for
America or has he become a puppet for Mr.
Obama? Mr. Obama personally campaigned
and signed the new START treaty with Russia.
The new START treaty is not good for
America. Some of the reasons that the new
START treaty is not good for America are
spelled out below.

This author was one of America's first international inspectors of disarmament and weapons systems when he was selected to participate in the First International Disarmament Event of 1968.

The work of this event was the foundation of the USA and Soviet Union disarmament treaties in the early 1970s.

The new START treaty was negotiated and signed by President Barack Obama with the Russian President Medevev under the direction of Vladimir Putin who by most watchers believe controls their government. The U. S. Senate has a legal obligation to "advise and consent" on any treaty that we agree to. Under the leadership of Senator John Kerry and Senator Richard Lugar the Senate's "advice" would not be accepted even though Senator Jon Kyl and others attempted to have some of the flaws in the treaty corrected. Senators Kerry and Lugar kept insisting that ANY CHANGE would require the treaty to be returned to the Russians and we couldn't take the risk of them getting upset and not agreeing to any change. The treaty was ratified by the

Democratic Party with every Democratic Senator voting for it along with 13 Republican Senators. A complete list of the Senators and their votes are included at the end of this section.

THIS VOTE ON THE NEW START TREATY MAY HAVE BEEN THE WEAKEST DISPLAY OF THE SENATE'S RESPONSIBILITY IN THE HISTORY OF THE UNITED STATES OF AMERICA WITH REGARDS TO A TREATY.

SEVERAL SENATORS IN THEIR TESTIMONY STATED THAT THE RUSSIANS HAVE CHEATED ON EVERY ARMS CONTROL TREATY WITH THE USA.

Keeping this in mind here are some of the flaws in this START treaty which weakens the USA.

For the first time in the history of our disarmament treaties with Russia this treaty "will not" have any inspectors on the ground.

Verification is the most important part of any disarmament treaty.

Former President Ronald Reagan said, "Trust and Verify". Verify every part of the treaty.

Senator Diane Feinstein said, "We have had two day inspections of the Russian nuclear weapons and missile arsenal". She proudly said that is sufficient time to do a complete intensive inspection.

The new START treaty allows 18 inspections a year. Does that mean 18 times two days or 36 days a year out of 365 days a year we are allowed inspections? This is insufficient time. Period.

This new START treaty by the insistence of the Russians has reduced the number of inspection sites in half from the last treaty to 35. These are the ONLY sites we can inspect. Russia is one of the largest countries in the world with an enormous land mass larger than the USA. There are parts of Russia where we are NOT allowed to go. We need access to all of Russia not just the designated areas mentioned in the START treaty. They could develop nuclear weapons and missiles without us knowing in these areas. Impossible you say? Are we depending on our satellites?

Response to this coming shortly.

First you don't need to be a mathematician to understand that if you have 35 sites and only 18 inspections a year each site will be inspected once every two years. That's not much verification, is it? But probably more devastating is that for the first time we need to give a 24 hour advance notice of our intent to inspect a particular site. WOW! Why have inspections if the Russians who have cheated on every arms control treaty with us can move their weapons systems. Twenty four hours is sufficient time to do this.

Remember we have no one on the ground for any surveillance.

HOW DUMB DO YOU HAVE TO BE TO AGREE TO THIS AND SIGN YOUR NAME TO THIS OR DO SOME OF THE SENATORS HAVE A DIFFERENT AGENDA? ISN'T PROTECTING THE USA THEIR NUMBER ONE PRIORITY?

Should the Senators who agreed to this be thrown out of office?

Back in the 1968 disarmament event we were on the ground "everyday" for six months. The "enemy" moved their assets, troops, and weapons systems every night over a 2000 mile area and we were to track and identify on a daily basis where everything was located.

Back to the satellite technology, how is that working for us? If the past year is any indication there is a lot we do not know and somehow our satellites didn't reveal to us. For example, North Korea revealed a secret new nuclear enrichment facility this past year to the shock of our intelligence services. Also, an Iranian watchdog group revealed a secret new facility in Iran approximately a year ago and on April 6, 2011 this group discovered another secret nuclear facility. We had no idea!

Going back to why we invaded Iraq our satellites revealed Saddam had weapons of mass destruction. How did that work out? Not only didn't our satellites reveal the above but our intelligence services didn't either.

President Obama wants to rely on our satellites and intelligence services to keep track of Russian's nuclear capability. Well the examples mentioned were NOT discovered so how accurate are we? Our national defense and survival is at stake.

Another flaw of the new START treaty is that the treaty does NOT allow us to improve our "current" missile defense. The Democratic senators state this limitation is not important even though several Russians including Putin have stated that this is vital to the treaty. Putin has indicated if the USA improves their missile defense they will pull out of the treaty and start developing more nuclear weapons. President Obama has already terminated our planned missile defense system in Poland and the Czech Republic because of Russian pressure. Secretary of Defense Robert Gates had previously indicated we need to improve our missile defense system.

This new START treaty is only about strategic nuclear weapons and does NOT include tactical nuclear weapons of which Russia has a 10-1 advantage. This is another major flaw. For example, among Russian's tactical nuclear weapons they have a submarine with a missile that has a range of 3000 miles. The USA is 3000 miles from the east coast to the west coast. Also a tactical nuclear weapon can be carried in a suitcase. They have 10,000 at last count.

The Democrats have said that is not important until we agree and ratify the strategic nuclear treaty first.

Negotiations are about leverage and positioning and we would be at a great disadvantage to negotiate a tactical nuclear treaty in the future having giving away so much in this treaty as there would be no incentive for the Russians to appease us. The author's experiences as a chief negotiator for industry wide management-labor contracts give him credibility about negotiations.

The only country that we have a disarmament treaty with is Russia.

We do not have a disarmament treaty with

Communist China, Pakistan, India, North Korea, Iran, France, Israel and Great Britain.

Senator John Kerry said that the USA and Russia have 90% of strategic nuclear weapons in the world. A look at the math indicates otherwise.

USA:	2200	Israel:	200
Russia:	1550	Pakistan:	100
China:	600	India:	100
Britain:	500	N. Korea:	5
France:	250	Iran:	?

According to the numbers there are 5,505 strategic nuclear weapons of which the USA and Russia have 3,750 – 68% of the total or approximately two-thirds. That assumes Canada and Australia do not have any which may not be correct.

The new START treaty requires the USA to reduce their strategic nuclear weapons from 2200 to 1550. Russia does not need to do any reductions thereby giving Russia an advantage of 10,000 tactical nuclear weapons to 1000 for the USA. MADNESS!

President Obama wants to reduce our nuclear weapons while the world is adding to theirs.

There is no reality to us reducing our nuclear strategic weapons and expecting the rest of the world to reduce theirs. I wrote my previous book, "It is Written the Shocking Downfall of the USA" based on our congress not facing reality and the downfall of the USA may become a reality.

All U.S. Senators take an oath of office to protect the United States of America from potential harm. The facts of this START treaty indicate it is flawed and yet the Democratic Senators voted along party lines to ratify it.

As I mentioned in my last book, even issues like national defense and national security are not above party politics.

LUCK IS NOT A VIABLE SUCCESSFUL STRATEGY FOR OUR NATIONAL DEFENSE AND NATIONAL SECURITY. If "luck" was a successful strategy Las Vegas would not exist.

THE UNITED STATES SENATE VOTE ON THE NEW START TREATY DECEMBER 22, 2010

YEAS BY DEMOCRATS/INDEPENDENTS

Akaka –HI

Baucus-MT

Bayh-IN

Begich-AK

Bennet-CO

Bingaman-NM

Boxer-CA

Brown-OH

Cantwell-WA

Cardin-MD

Carper-DE

Casey-PA

Conrad-ND

Coons-DE

Dodd-CT

Dorgan-ND

Durbin-IL

Feingold-WI

Warner-VA

Feinstein-CA

Franken-MN

Gillibrand-NY

Hagan-NC

Harkin-IA

Inouye-HI

Johnson-SD

Kerry-MA

Klobuchar-MN

Kohl-WI

Landrieu-LA

Lautenberg-NJ

Leahy-VT

Levin-MI

Lieberman-CT

Lincoln-AR

Manchin-WV

McCaskill-MO

Webb-VA

Menendez-NJ

Merkley-OR

Mikulski-MD

Murray-WA

Nelson-FL

Nelson-NE

Pryor-AR

Reed-RI

Reid-NV

Rockefeller-WV

Sanders-VT

Schumer-NY

Shaheen-NH

Specter-PA

Stabenow-MI

Tester-MT

Udall-CO

Udall-NM

Whitehouse-RI

Wyden-OR

YEAS BY REPUBLICANS

Alexander-TN
Bennett-UT
Brown-MA
Cochran-MS
Collins-ME

Corker-TN
Gregg-NH
Isakson-GA
Johanns-NE
Lugar-IN

Murkowski-AK
Snowe-ME
Voinovich-OH

NAYS BY REPUBLICANS

Barrasso-WY
Burr-NC
Chambliss-GA
Coburn-OK
Cornyn-TX
Crapo-ID
DeMint-SC
Ensign-NV
Enzi-WY

Graham-SC
Grassley-IA
Hatch-UT
Hutchison-TX
Inhofe-OK
Kirk-IL
Kyl-AZ
LeMieux-FL
McCain-AZ

McConnell-KY
Risch-ID
Roberts-KS
Sessions-AL
Shelby-AL
Thune-SD
Vitter-LA
Wicker-MS

NOT VOTING

Bond-MO

Brownback-KS

Bunning-KY

Ratified by 71 to 26 vote

THE TROJAN HORSE -- SYMBOL OF DECEPTION

The TROJAN HORSE is a tale from the Trojan
War. After a fruitless 10 year siege, the Greeks
constructed a huge wooden horse, (the horse
being the emblem of Troy) and hiding a select
force of 30 men inside, and fooling the Trojans
into wheeling the horse into their city as a
trophy. The Trojans having believed that the
Greeks had sailed away. That night the Greek
force crept out of the horse and opened the
gates to the city for the rest of the Greek army.
The Greek army entered and destroyed the
city of Troy, decisively ending the war.

THE MESSAGE OF THE STORY AND ITS RELEVANCE FOR TODAY

DECEPTION
ARE WE BEING DECEIVED BY THE PROGRESSIVE PARTY AND THEIR LEADERSHIP? IF THEY WON'T SIGNIFICANTLY REDUCE OUR DEBT AND DEFICIT YOU MAY HAVE YOUR ANSWER!

The Bible states that approximately 98% or 99% of the people will be DECEIVED at the end of time.

IS IT MUSLIM JIHAD?

The author listened to a discussion on the Muslim Brotherhood on C-SPAN ON March 21, 2011 presented by the Foundation for Defense of Democracies. The panel consisted of Cliff May, Lorenzo Vidino, Thomas Joscelyn and Reuel Marc Gerecht. All four were very experienced and knowledgeable about the Muslim Brotherhood. To briefly summarize their comments all four agreed that the older members of the Muslim Brotherhood still controlled the direction and the policies of the organization. The organization does have a central headquarters which was in Egypt and to some extent it appears is still there even after the downfall of Mubarak and the uprising. Mubarak who was not a member for the most part though his military and security forces kept the Muslim Brotherhood in check. The consensus was that the military would have to take over the leadership to keep order in the country and wait for the elections in the fall of 2011.

One comment was that the Muslim Brother-hood could garner 40% of the vote which would result in a large representation and possibly the largest of any group as the other political groups are not organized and financed. A variable is that in Egypt the Muslim Brotherhood dominates the labor unions. For the most part if an Egyptian wants to get a job or progress in his career the

Muslim Brotherhood has control of the work place. Therefore if an individual wants to work he must join the Muslim Brotherhood.

So the outcome of the election is unpredictable.

Years from now when the real history is written about Egypt and the Middle East there will be the discovery of how the labor unions played a role. American union leaders have influenced and trained the labor unions of the region for a number of years. It is easy to influence a group of people especially the 18-30 year olds who were on the outside looking in without a job to revolt under the deception of freedom. The unemployment rate of most of the countries in the Middle East for this group was approximately 40%.

A major point made by the panel was that Muslims who moved away from the Middle East to places like the USA and Europe were engaged in "double-talk". Publicly these Muslims state they are not a member of the Muslim Brotherhood and don't believe in that ideology but privately it appears that many do take part with some support. Many American and European Muslims regularly have taken trips to their Middle Eastern countries and have been spotted visiting the Muslim Brotherhood leaders.

Have you ever wondered why so many Muslims have moved to the USA in the last ten years since 9/11? Is it an organized migration to infiltrate? Remember the "Trojan horse"?

WHERE ARE THE AMERICAN WOMEN?

In the 1970s FEMINISM captured and dominated every part of American life. Women protested. Women burned their bras. Women roared and catapulted into American businesses and into the corporate boardrooms. Gloria Steinman was the focus of the women's movement. Women were VISIBLE everywhere and with a VOICE that permeated everything. Women gained power and

American would never be the same again.

In 2011 the Middle East came into world view. The Middle East controlled by Muslim dictators for the most part of the last 30/40 years found themselves in what appears to be a quest for individual freedom by their deprived citizens. Most of these Middle Eastern countries controlled their women by Sharia law. A law that requires a woman to be fully covered up except for the eyes. A law that if a woman is seen in public with a man other than her husband or family member she is subject to being stoned.

She may also be stoned if she cheats on her husband. Most of these countries restrict what kind of work a woman can do. Also, the family arranges the marriage and if the woman refuses she may be killed by her own family. If she becomes too westernized she could be punished.

As the 1970s turned into the 1980s and then the 1990s American women were still everywhere but they were satisfied, content with the progress they had made. They even made more money in some professions than men. They had accomplished their goal of getting a bigger "piece of the pie".

But they were SILENT to their Middle Eastern "sisters" who lived under Sharia law. The American women did not express themselves when it came to the plight of the Muslim women.

They exhibited no voice. There was no outrage even when some Muslim families who lived in the USA killed their own daughter because the family practiced Sharia.

Will American women wait until the Muslims in the USA gain some power and Sharia law is practiced in American communities before they speak out or will they be content with their own lives not to care? Some aspects of Sharia law is now practiced in some European countries including Great Britain. The odds are that America will follow what is happening in Europe.

WHERE IS THE POWER OF THE AMERICAN WOMEN?

SHOULD OUR LEADERS BE BRAVE AND DO THE SAME AS THE LEADER OF AUSTRALIA?

Julia Gillard, the Prime Minister of Australia, gave this speech.

Muslims who want to live under Islamic Sharia law, were told to get out of Australia, as the government targeted radicals in a bid to head off potential attacks.

"IMMIGRANTS, NOT AUSTRALIANS, MUST ADAPT. Take it or leave it. She is tired of this nation worrying about whether we are offending some individual or culture. Since the terrorist attacks on Bali, we have experienced a surge in patriotism by the majority of Australians."

"This culture has been developed over two centuries of struggles, trials, and victories by millions of men and women who have sought freedom."

"We speak mainly ENGLISH, not Spanish, Lebanese, Arabic, Chinese, Japanese, Russian, or any other language. Therefore, if you wish to become part of our society learn the language!"

"Most Australians believe in God. This is not some Christian, right wing, political push, but a fact, because Christian men and women, on Christian principles, founded this nation, and this is documented. It is certainly appropriate to display it on the walls of our schools. If God offends you, then she suggests you consider another part of the world as your new home because God is part of our culture."

"We will accept your beliefs, and will not question why. All we ask is that you accept ours, and live in harmony and peaceful enjoyment with us."

This is OUR COUNTRY, OUR LAND, AND OUR LIFESTYLE, and we will allow you every opportunity to enjoy all this. But once you are done complaining, whining, and griping about Our Flag, Our Pledge, Our Christian beliefs, or Our Way of Life, she highly encourages you to take advantage of one of our other great Australian freedoms, THE RIGHT TO LEAVE. We didn't force you to come here. You asked to be here. So accept the country you accepted."

Why should Americans adapt to all the foreigners that come to us shouldn't they adapt to America?

THE ENDINGS AND FINAL THOUGHT

ENDING NUMBER ONE!

You know a person by what he says, his writings and his actions.

If that person is a politician you can also know him by his votes and positions on the issues. You also can know a person by his history, his family, his friends, and associates. America can now define Barack Obama after his two plus years as our President.

In Obama's case many of his speeches and his public communications vastly differ from his actions. Many times he has said one thing but his actions have been the opposite. There has been a deception unparallel in an American President. The few short years that he was in the Illinois Senate he voted PRESENT so many times that either he couldn't make a decision or just wanted to be vague. The two years that he was in the U. S. Senate before running for the presidency he was rated as the most liberal senator.

We know about his family and what his father's ambitions were and how Barack has wanted to fulfill those. Obama's friends and associates have become legendary in their own right as many were the radicals of the 1960s. Some of them even have a history through their writings and actions of wanting to do HARM to America.

Obama's politics have become crystal clear to anyone who will take the time to look at his actions. Even after the November 2010 elections when the Democratic Party lost their overwhelming majority in the House of Representatives, Obama delivered an astonishing FY 2012 budget with a deficit of $1.65 Trillion Dollars. It is unimaginable that the Democratic Party wants to give the perception to the American people that they do not want to reduce our debt and deficit. As the Democratic Party controls the U. S. Senate and the White House they will thwart the efforts by the Republican Party to do the work of the American people.

The American people are fed up with the $1.5 Trillion Dollars deficit in FY 2011 and a projected $1.65 Trillion Dollars deficit in FY 2012 and an unsustainable federal deficit over $14 Trillion Dollars.

Forty-five of our fifty states have a budget in the red. One reason for this state debt is that the public sectors in the states have grown and with that their unfunded excessive pensions. The unions are calling the shots for the public sector employees. Already we have had demonstrations and near riots break out in Wisconsin, Ohio, and Indiana. This may be a harbinger of things to come. And these near riots may escalate into full blown riots as time goes by.

These possible riots which are led by the unions may include burning of buildings, shootings and killings as mobs may lead and dominate. Some union leaders have even called for violence. Picture this spreading all over the country. It may become large enough in the numbers of people involved that this may be described as America's Second Civil War.

READER THIS IS ENDING NUMBER ONE – YOU DECIDE THE FOLLOWING QUESTION.

The question is if there are riots, destruction of property, and shootings will President Obama call out the military to stop it as most of the rioters may be members of the union?

ENDING NUMBER TWO

President Obama in October 2012, a month before the 2012 presidential election, will take all of the Democratic Party Senators to the North Pole. They will each take off their shoes and dip their toes into the cold North Pole water for ten seconds. Obama will say," Aha". That will be their "Aha" moment. They will then return back to Washington, it's too cold to spend any more time there. President Obama will call a press conference and announce and promise that he and the Democratic Senators will cut the debt and deficit in half.

There will be celebrations all over the country. Obama will ride a white horse down Pennsylvania Avenue. The crowds will cheer.

Barack Obama will be re-elected.

READER THIS IS ENDING NUMBER TWO – YOU DECIDE THE FOLLOWING QUESTION.

WILL HE AND THEY KEEP THEIR PROMISES?

ENDING NUMBER THREE

The American experiment of individual freedom, equality, and capitalism was good but it also was responsible for the breeding for evil. The open society of individualism without the proper restraints resulted in a liberalism away from the WORD OF GOD and the TEN COMMANDMENTS. The greedy capitalism created the global economy and the communication systems like the internet, Facebook, and twitter may spur the uprisings of the people of the world to demand their piece of the pie.

When our CREATOR, GOD ALMIGHTY, created our world HE allowed the people to have a WILL of their own and that resulted in the irresponsibility of the masses as they got away from the service to HIM. GOD then asked the few faithful, Noah and his believers, to build an ark to save mankind from extinction. This act gave mankind a second chance.

In time GOD sent HIS SON, JESUS CHRIST, down to the earth to offer the people of the world an opportunity for salvation. JESUS was a JEW and HIS own people refused HIM. Then GOD took HIS favored nation status where HE protected the people away from the JEWS and they have suffered for centuries more than any other people. But GOD did not give up on the world. HE tried again to foster a religious and spiritual people.

A group of people left the "old world" to find a "new world" so they could worship GOD in freedom. This place became the United States of America. And it appears that GOD was pleased and therefore gave this new place HIS favored nation status. The astronomical odds against this new country surviving and prospering were overwhelming and only with GOD's HAND on her was she successful.

But the success, the power and the greed caused the people to turn away from GOD. Led by the DECEPTION of the leadership of the past Presidents, the Senate, the House of Representatives and the judges of the justice system this great experiment of America is on the verge of collapse and failure.

Americans created the promise of the global economy by building manufacturing plants all over the world. The backlash against establishing some controls against the greedy corporations will be astronomical but it's the ONLY way to save America and the rest of the world. We must create stability. But once they have experienced some prosperity and the hope of a better life it's hard to go back to what they had or didn't have. Sort of like once you have been to Paris it's hard to go back to the farm, or your former self as you have been transformed forever.

American women have spent billions of dollars over the years to look good and we men appreciate it, but if Sharia law takes over the only part of your body anyone will see are your eyes. What an OUTRAGE THAT THERE IS NO OUTRAGE OVER SHARIA LAW BY AMERICAN WOMEN. I suggest you study Sharia law. American women you are the backbone of America and if you were to decide to take action the men will follow. You will need to act and vote for the conservative party who wants to protect you and save America.

Under the guise of freedom the peoples of the Middle East have started an upheaval that has overthrown their masters. This movement in time may be consumed by the JIHAD. The engine that allows the world to function in 2011 and beyond is oil/gas. Once the JIHAD is in control of most of the world's supply the economies of the world will falter. The USA, China, India, Europe, and Japan are heavily depended on this resource.

The BIBLE talks about the DECEPTION of the LAST DAYS. Almost every person on earth will be DECEIVED by the new power of evil. That's 98% to 99% of all peoples. The JIHAD of the ISLAMIC RELIGION states that there will be ONLY one religion that dominates the world at the end and if one does not convert to it they will be killed. The only religion that has this mandate is the radical part of the Islamic religion. So people of the world you can accept this fate without a fight and go like sheep to be slaughtered or you can change the dynamic of this prophecy. GOD is waiting for HIS people to act. GOD may have mercy on the world if enough people return to worship HIM.

READER THIS IS ENDING NUMBER THREE – YOU DECIDE IS OUR DEMOCRACY SAFE WITH OUR PRESENT VALUES?

FINAL THOUGHT

A DEMOCRACY CANNOT EXIST OR
CONTINUE TO EXIST UNLESS THE
MAJORITY OF PEOPLE HAVE CHRISTIAN
VALUES. OUR FOUNDING FATHERS
REALIZED THIS.

In Europe church attendance and people
believing in GOD is dramatically down – only
about 20% of the people now call themselves
Christians. The main cause is lack of accepting
responsibility and depending on the government to give them a monthly welfare check.
Marriage rates are down, honesty is lacking,
crime is up, and people are not industrious --
they don't want to work.

This same phenomenon is happening in the
USA. Statistics now indicate that 21% of
Americans are atheists up from 4% in 1960.
Approximately 40% do not confess to being a
Christian. Over 40% of Americans receive
some kind of monthly assistance from the
federal government. It's a breakdown of our

society as the federal government has overreached into our daily lives and now we are too dependent on it. Americans are not as self reliant and responsible as they were in 1960. People don't want to take responsibility for themselves.

As of the date of publishing this book the national deficit is $14,300,000,000,000. Six months from now in October 2011 the national deficit will be $15,300,000,000,000 as President Obama will add another trillion dollars. If things don't change and we don't reduce our national deficit our national deficit will be over twenty trillion dollars by 2020. When politicians talk about the deficit, they talk as if their only concern is their children and grandchildren when in fact, today's adults are affected as we will be at 100% of GDP in a year. Politicians need to stress more urgency as the reality may be the children and grand-children could be 20 years away from being on their own. The fact is none of us, except the rich, will continue to have it possibly as early as a year from now.

The fact is that the "super rich" do not create most of the new jobs in the USA. Small businesses do! Approximately 70% of new jobs created in the USA are created by small businesses. Therefore, reality is if the huge tax breaks for the "super rich" are reduced it should not have a major negative impact on the economy. Actually it should improve our economy.

Will you stand up to reduce our national debt and deficit?

As a registered independent voter I tried to make a responsible attempt at solving our national debt and deficit. It was not my attempt to portray Obama in a negative way. Reality is Obama through his liberal progressive policies has put himself in a negative way as he has added $5 Trillion Dollars to the national deficit in approximately 2 ½ years as President. From George Washington to George W. Bush, all the presidents combined did not total the amount of deficit that Obama has. The workload of the federal government has not increased so why has Obama hired over 200,000 new federal employees?

GOD'S GIFT TO US IS LIFE. OUR GIFT
TO GOD IS WHAT WE BECOME. GOD
MEASURES OUR SUCCESS IN OUR
CHARACTER, OUR VALUES, OUR
STANDARDS, OUR BELIEFS,
AND NOT IN HOW MUCH MONEY WE
HAVE ACQUIRED.

ABOUT THE AUTHOR

Roger Ewing has a Bachelor's Degree from Bowling Green State University in Ohio. He received a Master's Degree from the University of Southern California and did his PhD work at Arizona State University. Roger was an Air Force Officer and a Management Consultant for many years. He currently rescues and finds homes for Saint Bernard dogs.

RESCUING AMERICA

It has been documented that SAINT BERNARDS have rescued and saved the lives of over 1000 people. THE SAINT BERNARD IS THE SYMBOL FOR RESCUE. Roger Ewing is attempting to rescue and save the American people and the United States of America.

www.ingramcontent.com/pod-product-compliance
Lightning Source LLC
Chambersburg PA
CBHW070139290526
45789CB00002B/547